NEW WORLDS

BY JOHN HAMILTON

VISIT US AT

WWW.ABDOPUBLISHING.COM

Published by ABDO Publishing Company, 4940 Viking Drive, Suite 622, Edina, Minnesota 55435.
Copyright ©2007 by Abdo Consulting Group, Inc. International copyrights reserved in all countries.
No part of this book may be reproduced in any form without written permission from the publisher.
ABDO & Daughters™ is a trademark and logo of ABDO Publishing Company.

Printed in the United States.

Editor: Paul Joseph
Graphic Design: John Hamilton
Cover Design: Neil Klinepier
Cover Illustration: *Cyteen III* ©1988 Don Maitz
Interior Photos and Illustrations: p 1 alien landscape, Corbis; p 4 cover of *Hyperion*, courtesy Bantam
Spectra; p 5 *Escape From Below* ©1989 Don Maitz; pp 6-7 *The Island of Dr. Death* ©1979 Don Maitz;
p 8 illustration from *Harmonia Macrocosmica*, Corbis; p 9 Earth and moon, NASA; pp 10-11 montage of
planets, NASA; p 12 *Last Run on Venus*, Mary Evans Picture Library; p 13 surface of Venus, NASA;
p 14 illustration from *War of the Worlds*, Mary Evans Picture Library; p 15 *Thuvia, Maid of Mars*;
p 16 two Earth-like worlds, Corbis; p 17 *Checkout the Sunset* ©1978 Don Maitz; p 18 Mars and Earth,
Corbis; p 19 *Interstellar Fuel*, ©1979 Janny Wurts; pp 20-21 life on alien planet, Corbis; p 22 cover of
Red Mars, courtesy Bantam Spectra; p 23 *Space Series B*, ©1981 Don Maitz; p 24 (top) Mars terraformed,
NASA, John Hamilton; p 24 (bottom) red and green terraces, Corbis; p 25 *Thrilling Wonder Stories*, Mary
Evans Picture Library; p 26 astronauts in International Space Station, Corbis; p 27 *Cyteen III* ©1988 Don
Maitz; p 28 *Ringworld Throne*, courtesy Del Ray; p 29 International Space Station in orbit, NASA.

Library of Congress Cataloging-in-Publication Data

Hamilton, John, 1959-
  New worlds / John Hamilton.
     p. cm. -- (The world of science fiction)
  Includes bibliographical references and index.
  ISBN-13: 978-1-59679-991-2
  ISBN-10: 1-59679-991-9
  1. Science fiction--History and criticism--Juvenile literature. I. Title. II. Series: Hamilton, John, 1959-
World of science fiction.

PN3433.5.H36 2007
809.3'8762--dc22

                              2006016393

CONTENTS

DISTANT
HORIZONS

"To seek out strange new worlds…"
—from *Star Trek*

"At last, unable to go further, they paused behind the last living tree near them and stared out over the awful panorama spread before them. Directly in front, a vast puffball, its pocked, white circumference many yards in diameter, reared up in bloated isolation. … There was no normal growth in view, not even grass, nor any bare ground not covered by some slime or smear of leprous muck."
—from *Hiero's Journey* by Sterling E. Lanier

"It had been a warm, rainy day in Keats, Hyperion's capital, and even after the rains stopped a layer of clouds moved slow and heavy over the city, filling the air with the salt scent of the ocean twenty kilometers to the west. … The clouds glowed blue-white. Half a minute later an ebony spacecraft broke through the overcast and descended carefully on a tail of fusion flame, its navigation lights blinking red and green against the grey."
—from *Hyperion* by Dan Simmons

Facing page: Escape From Below, by Don Maitz.
Below: The cover of Dan Simmons' novel, *Hyperion*.

An astronaut unseals his capsule and steps onto a new planet, gazing upward. Multiple moons streak across the heavens. Thick, honey-scented air greets his nostrils. He hears great beasts wading through primeval swamps, and sees ferns towering hundreds of feet toward a blood-red sky. Where in the world are we? Or, as a science-fiction author would say, where in the universe?

Setting, where a story's action takes place, is extremely important in science fiction. A proper setting helps give the reader a sense of wonder, one of the hallmarks of good science fiction. For the author or filmmaker, it's a tricky task. You need to create that sense of wonder by making your setting different from Earth—often quite a bit different. If there are two suns burning in the sky, you know for certain you are somewhere special, beyond our world.

On the other hand, if you make your new world *too* weird, with everything mixed up and turned upside down, the reader won't take your story seriously. You have to maintain a certain taste of reality. This is called verisimilitude. The world must at least have the *appearance* of being true to life. The reader has to wonder, *could this place really be out there, somewhere among the stars?*

Science fiction authors call this process "world-building." It's a method of making a story's setting scientifically plausible, so that the details make sense. It can involve a lot of research. Writers have to know a lot about science, especially astronomy, geology, and biology. But once you know what's *possible*, you can wrap your story around that made-up world. For example, if a story has creatures made of lava and rock, it would make sense to have them live on a planet with many active volcanoes.

Including real science in a science fiction story: you might say, "well, duh!" But some writers resist world-building, fearing it will stunt their creativity. They don't understand that world-building is not a straightjacket. It provides a background, a framework, for good science fiction. Science doesn't overwhelm a story, it supports it. Done right, a well-researched setting will, as if by magic, transport the reader into a new world. It's a fun way of storytelling, where anything might happen—and probably will.

Right: The Island of Dr. Death, by artist Don Maitz.

7

THE SOLAR SYSTEM

In the beginning, there was only one world: Earth. There were no stars. People saw only pinpricks of light in the night sky. Before the Age of Reason, when science was in its infancy, nobody knew that the universe held trillions of fiery suns, or that countless new planets might orbit them. People looked up and merely saw bright, twinkling lights set against blackness. Some of those lights moved differently than the rest. People watched them, plotted their movements, and called them planets. They were given names, such as Mars or Jupiter, but the planets weren't thought of as new worlds.

In 1543, Polish astronomer Nicolaus Copernicus published his observation that the earth and other planets of the solar system orbited the Sun. It was a radical view that turned the science of astronomy upside down. Until that time, most people believed the earth was the center of the universe, that all other heavenly bodies orbited our world, the only world in which life could possibly exist.

Right: A Copernican sun-centered model of the solar system, in an atlas called *Harmonia Macrocosmica*, published in 1661 by Andreas Cellarius.
Facing page: Moonrise over Earth, as seen from the Space Shuttle in orbit.

In the early 17th century, Italian scientist Galileo Galilei turned his new and improved telescopes on the Moon and planets of our solar system, as well as the stars of the Milky Way. He discovered mountains on Earth's Moon, sunspots, and several moons orbiting the gas giant Jupiter. These were not mere lights in the sky—they were whole new worlds, radically different from Earth.

Combining Coperincus' and Galileo's discoveries, people started thinking that there actually could be life beyond our own Earth. In 1698, astronomer Christiaan Huygens wrote a book, *Cosmotheoros*, which explored the possibility of alien life on other planets. Half a century later, the French writer Voltaire published *Micromegas* in 1752. It told the story of a giant from the star Sirius who visits Earth.

When science fiction stories became widely popular in the late 19th and early 20th centuries, Earth's Moon was the most common other-worldly destination. Authors Jules Verne and H. G. Wells each wrote tales of lunar exploration. Wells' 1901 novel, *The First Men in The Moon*, tells of two astronauts who travel to the Moon and find a bleak, lifeless landscape. But as the Sun rises, fast-growing plants suddenly sprout and spread. The two explorers get lost in a jungle, and then encounter an alien civilization called the Selenites. These strange, insect-like Moon people live underground. The two Earthmen are captured, but after a time escape by overpowering the Selenites. (Since the Moon's gravity is much weaker than Earth's, the insect-people have evolved puny muscles.) One of the astronauts escapes in the spaceship and returns home, but the other is recaptured by the Selenites and is doomed to live with them for the rest of his days on the Moon.

Right: A montage of nine planets and four large moons of Jupiter photographed by NASA's planetary missions. The Rosette Nebula is in the background.

By the end of the 19th century, astronomers using bigger and more powerful telescopes could see mountains and other surface features on the planets. As our knowledge of these other worlds grew, they became tempting subjects for science fiction. The two most common settings were Mars and Venus, our nearest neighbors in the solar system. The other planets, such as the gas giants Jupiter and Saturn, the icy outer worlds such as Pluto, or the fiery Sun-kissing Mercury, seemed too harsh to support life. There are certainly many stories that take place on these planets, but they are almost always about the challenges of Earthlings trying to settle in these harsh, inhospitable worlds.

Today, using robotic space probes and powerful telescopes, we have a very good idea what the surfaces of the planets look like, and just how hazardous they would be for humans. But in the early days of astronomy, there was a lot of guesswork. Venus, which is about the same size as Earth, seemed to have a perpetual cloud cover. What was hidden underneath? Some speculated that the clouds hovered over a vast system of rainforests. In Edgar Rice Burroughs' *Venus* series of books, published from 1934 to 1946, a human-like race of aliens live in a lush, jungle world they call Amtor. In 1943, C. S. Lewis published *Perelandra*, which takes place on a Venus that resembles the Garden of Eden. Author Leigh Brackett wrote several short stories that take place on a warm, wet Venus that is filled with oceans and swamps. Today, of course, we know that Venus has a poisonous atmosphere of carbon dioxide, with a greenhouse effect so terrible that the surface temperature is hot enough to melt lead.

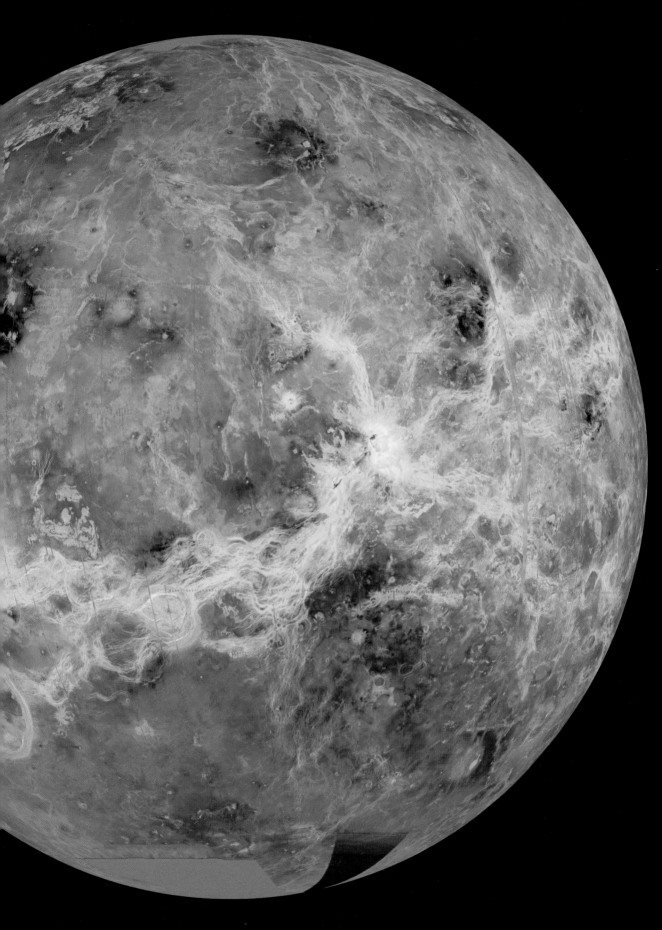

Of all the planets besides Earth, Mars was the most popular subject for science fiction writers. Scientific discoveries made it an exciting place. Using powerful telescopes, astronomers such as Giovanni Schiaparelli and Percival Lowell made some of the first maps of the Red Planet. They observed gigantic volcanoes, miles-deep canyons, even a crisscross network of "canals," which many thought were dug by an alien civilization.

These observations fired the imagination of a generation of science fiction writers. H. G. Wells practically invented the alien-invasion story with his army of heat-ray-toting Martians in 1898's *The War of the Worlds*. In 1911's *A Princess of Mars*, Edgar Rice Burroughs transports his hero, John Carter, to the Red Planet, where the four-armed inhabitants call their world Barsoom. Carter battles the warlike creatures using his great strength, which he receives because of Mars' lesser gravity. Olaf Stapledon's *Last and First Men*, published in 1930, is a future history of Earth that includes several Martian invasions. In *The Martian Chronicles*, Ray Bradbury's 1950 masterpiece, the tables are turned: a dying race of intelligent Martians is threatened by arrogant Earthlings who colonize the Red Planet.

Some of the most famous names in science fiction, from Arthur C. Clarke and Robert Heinlein, to Isaac Asimov and Kim Stanley Robinson, have set their stories on Mars. Today, thanks to several NASA space probes and robotic landers, we know that Mars is a cold, barren place with an atmosphere as thin as a ghost. It's a dried-out world, a disappointment to writers who dreamed that, perhaps, we would discover a sister Earth, and maybe even alien life. But Mars continues to fascinate, even today. Dan Simmons' epic 2003 novel, *Illium*, and its 2005 sequel, *Olympos*, both have major action that takes place on Mars. The Red Planet's appeal, it seems, is as strong as ever.

Facing page: An illustration from the 1906 edition of H. G. Wells' *The War of the Worlds. Below:* The cover of Edgar Rice Burroughs' *Thuvia, Maid of Mars.*

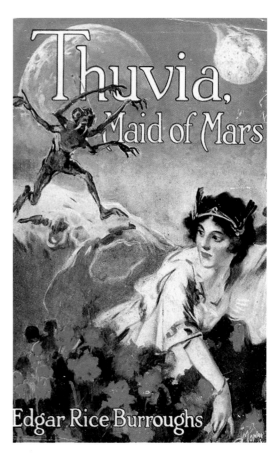

ALIEN WORLDS

Sometimes, reality stinks. During the second half of the 20th century, as modern astronomy began unraveling the mysteries of the solar system, it became obvious that Earth was the only planet in the neighborhood capable of sustaining life. So much for Martians, or jungles on Venus. But instead of accepting defeat, science fiction writers and filmmakers packed up their bags and moved to galaxies far, far away.

Worlds that orbit stars other than our own are called extrasolar planets. By venturing beyond our solar system, science fiction writers free themselves to describe any kind of planet they want to. The range of new worlds in science fiction is staggering. Some are big, some are small. There are planets with crushing gravity, or with almost no gravity at all. Some planets are truly exotic, orbiting binary suns or containing seas of molten gold.

In hard science fiction, however, reality must be met head-on, and most writers take pains to make their fictional worlds as realistic as possible. If a planet orbits close to a large sun, a red giant perhaps, naturally the surface temperature of the planet will be blazing hot. Multiple moons? Fine, but the increased tidal forces will wreak havoc on the planet's oceans, if it has any. These kinds of questions are often worked out in great detail by many science fiction writers even before they begin plotting their story or creating their characters. In fact, in hard science fiction, the setting is often considered a character itself.

Right: Two Earth-like worlds revolving around an alien sun.
Facing page: Checkout the Sunset, by Don Maitz.

© Don Maitz 78

Not all science fiction is "hard," where reality reigns supreme. Some types of science fiction, like *space opera*, emphasize adventure, bizarre places, and colorful characters. The *Star Wars* movies are one example. In these kinds of tales, the fictional worlds are limited only by the author's imagination.

Since most science fiction stories are about human beings, many fictional planets are much the same as Earth—they have plenty of oxygen, water, and geographic similarities, such as rocky mountains or high plains. Having an Earth-similar planet lets the characters get out of their bulky spacesuits, which can be a hindrance to the action of the story. Sometimes these kinds of planets are called "Earth clones." In the *Star Trek* universe, planets are classified by type. If a new world is similar to Earth, it is called a "Class M" planet.

Just because a planet is "Earth like" doesn't mean it has to be *exactly* like Earth. In fact, there are probably striking differences. Earth's tilt gives us our four seasons. An extrasolar planet might not be tilted at all, which would mean no seasons. Or an extreme tilt, combined with a slow rotation, might result in wild weather and climate patterns. The new world might also have a different-colored sky, depending on how the sunrays reflect through the alien atmosphere.

Facing page: Interstellar Fuel Station, by Janny Wurts.
Below: The planet Mars, with Earth in the background.

If a science fiction story involves an extrasolar planet, and it's not an Earth clone, then it's usually one of two types: a rocky planet or a gas giant. A rocky planet (which includes most moons) is sort of like Earth, but life hasn't taken hold for various reasons, such as a lack of atmosphere, crushing gravity, or no water. A good example of a rocky planet from our own solar system would be Mars.

A gas giant, on the other hand, is a seething, whirling caldron of gasses, such as hydrogen and helium, with a superheated core. Some people think hydrogen-breathing creatures might exist on gas giants, floating their entire lives in turbulent layers of hot gasses.

More likely, however, would be oxygen-breathing creatures living on an Earth-like moon orbiting a gas giant. In our own solar system, gas giants have many moons. Io and Europa are two of Jupiter's largest satellites. They hold hints of the right materials needed for life as we know it: liquid water and oxygen. Titan, the largest of Saturn's moons (slightly larger than the planet Mercury), is the only known moon in our solar system that has a developed atmosphere. In Titan's case, the atmosphere is made mostly of nitrogen and methane, with no oxygen. But the very existence of Titan's atmosphere gives science fiction writers hope that, somewhere out there, exists a moon that can support life. The possibilities are endless.

Right: Life sprouts on an alien landscape.

TERRAFORMED PLANETS

Terraforming is a word that means, "Earth shaping." It's a way of turning a desolate planet into an Earth-like world that people can live on. It's obviously never been done before, but science fiction writers and real-life engineers have been thinking for years of ways to make alien planets livable. It would be an extremely difficult task and take a long time, perhaps hundreds or even thousands of years. But terraforming presents an exciting possibility: if we ever use up Earth's resources, can we simply manufacture a new planet and move?

The term "terraforming" first appeared in Jack Williamson's 1949 science fiction novel, *Seetee Shock*. But it's an idea that's much older. *Last and First Men*, a famous 1930 novel by Olaf Stapledon, told of humans terraforming Venus. In 1961, astronomer Carl Sagan wrote an influential paper detailing how Venus could be made livable by seeding the atmosphere with algae, which would scrub out the deadly levels of carbon dioxide in the planet's air. We know today that this plan wouldn't work, but Sagan's paper gave many people ideas about how to alter alien climates.

Terraforming concepts have also been used in science fiction films. In the 1986 movie *Aliens*, humans build a "shake-and-bake" colony, where huge machines spew gasses into the air to make the atmosphere of planet LV-426 breathable by humans. The terraforming process in *Aliens* takes decades, but in the 1990 film *Total Recall*, alien technology transforms the Martian ecosystem in a matter of minutes.

In real life, of all the planets in our solar system, Mars is the most likely candidate for terraforming. The frozen, dead planet has been the subject of many stories about planetary engineering. The most popular is a series of three books by science fiction writer Kim Stanley Robinson. His novels, *Red Mars* (1992), *Green Mars* (1993), and *Blue Mars* (1996), chronicle the human colonizing and terraforming of Earth's neighbor.

Facing page: Space Series B, by Don Maitz.
Below: The book cover of Kim Stanley Robinson's *Red Mars.*

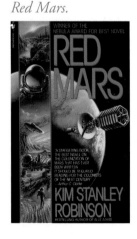

Terraforming Mars is a good example of the challenges humans would face in making any planet livable. On the Red Planet, the two biggest tasks would be making the air breathable and providing enough heat so that future colonists wouldn't freeze to death. One way of doing this would be to place huge microwave generators in orbit around Mars, and then bombard the planet's surface with heat-generating microwaves. Eventually, water trapped in the soil would be released into the thin Martian atmosphere. The water vapor would create a greenhouse effect, helping speed the planet's warming. The thickening of the atmosphere would also speed the formation of gasses needed to create oxygen. Or, the needed gasses could be imported from elsewhere, such as the hydrogen- and oxygen-rich moons orbiting Jupiter or Saturn.

Obviously, terraforming an entire planet such as Mars would be frighteningly expensive, and there would be many technical problems to overcome. In addition to these hurdles, there are ethical issues to be reckoned with as well. Is it right to destroy a planet's entire ecosystem just so humans can live there? And what if we accidentally wipe out previously unknown alien life-forms?

Despite the difficulties, creating a human-friendly planet from scratch is a thrilling prospect. If the technical details can be solved, and the ethical questions answered, terraforming an alien planet might well be humanity's greatest achievement.

Above: An artist's conception of Mars being terraformed.
Facing page: The February 1938 issue of *Thrilling Wonder Stories* shows a spaceship using a heat ray to melt Mars' polar ice cap.
Below: Could humans someday terraform Mars?

GIANT AND DWARF STARS By SIR JAMES JEANS

THRILLING
WONDER
STORIES

FEB.

15¢

A THRILLING
PUBLICATION

LIFE ETERNAL
A Novelette of
Solar Secrets
By EANDO
BINDER

DREAM-DUST
FROM MARS
A Novelette of
The Future
By MANLY
WADE WELLMAN
•
ZONES OF
SPACE
A Novelette of
the Sunken World
By MAX C. SHERIDAN

LIVING IN SPACE

Planets and moons aren't the only new worlds explored in science fiction. Sometimes the "worlds" are entirely man-made. These artificial megastructures are so huge that people living inside often forget they're not living on an actual planet. Some science fiction stories feature "cities in space," in which citizens form their own governments and societies, completely separate from the planet below.

Space stations are the most common kind of artificial worlds in science fiction. Like spaceships, there are several real-life examples, although space stations today are much smaller than those envisioned by science fiction authors and filmmakers. In years past, Russia has had great success with its Salyut and Mir space stations. In the 1970s, the United States built its Skylab space station. The Salyut and Skylab space stations were launched in one piece. Mir was built over time by launching several modular pieces and then assembling them in orbit.

The largest space station ever built is the International Space Station (ISS), which is a joint project between several countries,

Facing page: Cyteen III, by Don Maitz. *Below:* An artist's conception of astronauts working inside the International Space Station.

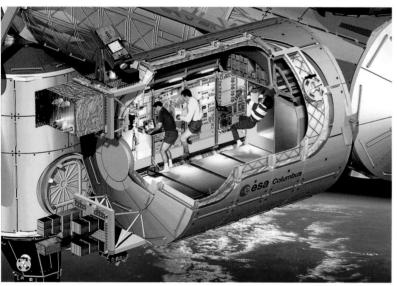

including the United States, Russia, Japan, Canada, Brazil, plus member countries of the European Space Agency. The ISS will take many years and billions of dollars to complete. Dozens of Space Shuttle launches will be required to get all the pieces into orbit.

When finished, the International Space Station will have 10 main pressurized modules in which up to six astronauts will live and work in the weightlessness of space.

Unlike spaceships, space stations have no propulsion system. They're like giant office buildings, or even small cities, usually built in low planetary orbit. Some fictional space stations, like the one in *2001: A Space Odyssey*, are ring-shaped, revolving to provide the inhabitants with artificial gravity. Others are giant, hollow cylinders, like the mysterious alien craft in Arthur C. Clarke's 1972 novel, *Rendezvous with Rama*. Unlike space stations that orbit planets, the craft in *Rendezvous with Rama* traveled through deep space. Like a ring-shaped space station, however, it also rotated, creating an Earth-like gravitational field. Space stations can also resemble enormous spheres, like the Death Star from *Star Wars*. Space stations have been featured in many other novels, movies, and television shows, including *Babylon 5* and *Star Trek: Deep Space Nine*.

Several other types of megastructures are sometimes featured in science fiction tales. An orbital is a ring-shaped artificial habitat, bigger than a space station, that spins to provide gravity. Sometimes called "god's bracelet," an orbital can hold thousands of people and contain many types of habitats inside its shell, including oceans and deserts. The Xbox video game *Halo* is set in an orbital built by an alien race called the Forerunners.

On an even larger scale, some ringed habitats completely encircle their home planets, such as the p- and e-rings in Dan Simmons' 2003 novel, *Illium*. In 1970, author Larry Niven published *Ringworld*, the first of his *Known Space* books. *Ringworld* envisions a mind-bogglingly large alien megastructure, an artificial ring one million miles (1.6 million km) wide that circles a star. The ring has an orbital circumference of 600 million miles (965,606,400 km). With inner walls over 1,000 miles (1.6 thousand km) tall, the inside of the ring has the same surface area as three million Earth-size planets. *Ringworld* tells the story of four human explorers who crash-land on the ring, then set out to explore it and unlock its mysteries. *Ringworld* was a very popular book, which led to three sequels. In 1970 and 1971, it won both the Hugo and Nebula Awards, science fiction's highest honor.

Facing page: The International Space Station is backdropped against a cloud-covered part of Earth, as the orbital outpost drifts away from the Space Shuttle *Discovery* on August 6, 2005. *Below:* The cover of Larry Niven's *Ringworld Throne*, a sequel to his popular novel, *Ringworld*.

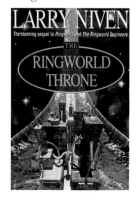

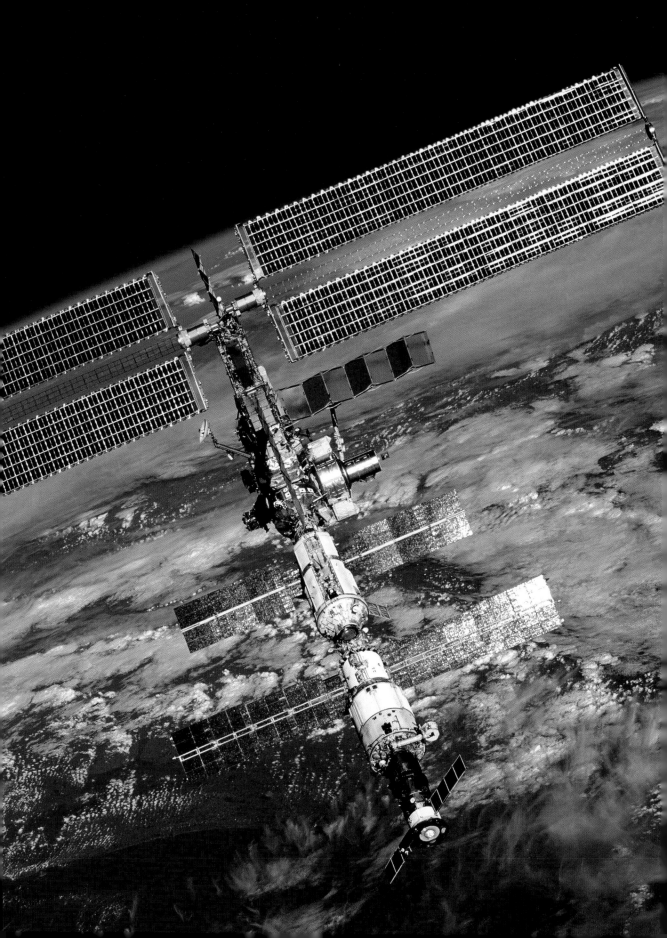

GLOSSARY

AGE OF REASON

A time in the 18th century, especially in Europe, when people began to believe that they could think, or reason, to discover truth, and to shape society. The rising importance of science played a big part in the Age of Reason. Before this time, many societies were formed by religions, or superstitions.

ASTRONOMY

The scientific study of the universe, including the stars and planets, how they were formed, how they move, and their composition and size.

EARTHLING

An inhabitant of the planet Earth. In science fiction, an alien might call a human being an Earthling.

EXTRASOLAR

An object, such as a planet or asteroid, that orbits a sun other than our own.

GREENHOUSE EFFECT

A trapping of the Sun's heat in a planet's atmosphere, similar to the heat build-up caused by the panes of glass in a greenhouse.

HUGO AWARD

The annual award presented by the World Science Fiction Society to honor the year's best science fiction. Named after the legendary writer and editor Hugo Gernsback, who founded *Amazing Stories* (left) in 1926.

NASA

The National Aeronautics and Space Administration. NASA is the United States' main space agency, responsible for programs such as the Space Shuttle and unmanned space probes.

Nebula

A cloud of dust or gas in outer space. Nebulas, such as the one at the top of this page, are usually seen as bright, glowing patches set against the night sky.

Nebula Award

The prestigious annual award presented by the Science Fiction Writers of America (SFWA) for excellence in science fiction writing.

Solar System

The collection of planets, asteroids, and comets that orbit the Sun. The solar system includes nine recognized planets: Mercury, Venus, Earth, Mars, Jupiter, Saturn, Uranus, Neptune, and Pluto.

Space Opera

A type of science fiction that emphasizes strong characters, a sense of wonder, and non-stop action and adventure. *Star Wars* is a good example of modern space opera. Space opera usually takes place on distant planets, featuring spaceships that can quickly travel between the stars. The term was probably coined in 1941 by author Wilson Tucker, as a play on the terms "horse opera" (Westerns) and "soap opera."

Terraform

To make an alien planet more like Earth. In science fiction, terraforming is usually achieved with high technology, such as by "seeding" clouds with special chemicals to make them produce oxygen, so that future colonists can live on the planet.

Verisimilitude

Something that has the appearance of being true, or real.

INDEX